11/98-12
8/00-15 7/10/00

JAN 1995

BRAHMS

In loving memory of Perle and George

First edition for the United States, Canada,
and the Philippines published 1993
by Barron's Educational Series, Inc.

Design David West Children's Book Design

© Copyright by Aladdin Books Ltd 1993
Copyright in the text © Ann Rachlin / Fun with Music

Designed and produced by
Aladdin Books Ltd
28 Percy Street
London W1P 9FF

All inquiries should be addressed to:
Barron's Educational Series, Inc.
250 Wireless Boulevard
Hauppauge, NY 11788

International Standard Book No. 0-8120-1542-8

Library of Congress Catalog Card No. 92-32177

Library of Congress Cataloging-in-Publication Data
Rachlin, Ann.
        Brahms / by Ann Rachlin ; illustrated by Susan Hellard.
            p. cm. -- (Famous children)
        Summary: A biography of the nineteenth-century German composer
with emphasis on his childhood and early musical training.
    ISBN 0-8120-1542-8
    1. Brahms, Johannes, 1833-1897 – Childhood and youth – Juvenile
literature. 2. Composers – Germany – Biography – Juvenile literature.
    [1. Brahms, Johannes, 1833-1897–Childhood and youth.
    2. Composers.] I. Hellard, Susan, ill. II. Title.III. Series:
Rachlin, Ann. Famous children.
ML3930.B75R3 1993
780'.92--dc20
[B]   92-32177
                                                                      CIP
                                                                  AC MN

Printed in Belgium
3456 987654321

Famous Children

BRAHMS

A<small>NN</small> R<small>ACHLIN</small>
<small>ILLUSTRATED BY</small> S<small>USAN</small> H<small>ELLARD</small>

BARRON'S

Tin soldiers were the only toys Johannes Brahms had. They lay in a box on the floor but he kept his precious flute under his pillow. It was 1839. Johannes lived with his brother and sister and father and mother in three rooms in a tall wooden house on Ulricus Street in the ancient German city of Hamburg. They were very poor and shared their house with many other families.

One morning the sound of music woke Johannes. From his window he could see Fritz the organ-grinder coming down the street. All the neighborhood children came running out to listen to the catchy tunes of the barrel organ. Fritz's pet monkey danced in time to the music and took coins from the children to give to his master. Johannes threw on his clothes and dashed downstairs to join the fun.

When the music was over, Johannes raced back up the stairs. Leaping onto his bed he took his flute from under the pillow and began to play all the tunes that he had heard on the barrel organ.

"Just listen, Jakob," said his mother. "He hears a tune and he can play it immediately."

"Yes," said Mr. Brahms. "Soon he will be able to play his flute and violin for the sailors on the waterfront. That'll bring in some extra money." Mrs. Brahms sighed. Her husband worked hard but earned only a few pennies playing the double bass in cafes and inns. There was never enough money. But Mrs. Brahms did not like the thought of her little boy playing for rough sailors in those noisy inns at the harbor. After all he was only six.

Johannes's father came to the bedroom door.

"That was very good, Johannes. Would you like to play your flute for one of my musician friends?"

"Is he the one who has a piano, Father? Do you think he'll let me try it?" His father frowned.

"No, I do not," he answered sternly. "Forget the piano, Johannes. Pianos are for rich people."

At his house, father's friend smiled kindly at Johannes. But Johannes was not looking. He was staring at the piano. He walked quietly over to it while the two men were talking. He was just lifting up his hand to touch the keys when his father's voice rang out.

"Come away from there, Johannes. It's time to play your flute."

The last note died away and Johannes looked up at his father's friend.

"Your boy is very musical, Jakob," he said. "He should have lessons."

"How would I pay?" cried Mr. Brahms. "I have barely enough money for food." Johannes tiptoed toward the piano again.

"Come away!" His father sounded angry.

"He can't do any harm, Jakob. Look at the keys, Johannes. I will tell you the names of the notes."

"No need, sir," replied Johannes. "I can tell all the notes when I hear them."

The two men stared at each other. Could this be true? Mr. Brahms turned Johannes around so that his back was to the piano. His friend played a note.

"F," said Johannes. They tried another key.

"B flat," said Johannes, without hesitating.

"Your son has perfect pitch, Jakob. It is a rare gift. You must take him to see Otto Cossel at once. He is a fine teacher. He will know what is best for Johannes."

"There's no way..." said Jakob to his wife. "We just can't afford music lessons." Mrs. Brahms looked thoughtful.

"It's a shame, Jakob. He thinks only of the piano. Take him to Mr. Cossel. See what he has to say."

"Your son is seven you say? Mmmmmm." Mr. Cossel stroked his chin.

"Well, Johannes Brahms, would you like me to teach you how to play the piano?" Johannes could not believe his ears.

"But we have no money, sir," cried Mr. Brahms. "No piano either."

"Johannes is very gifted," said Mr. Cossel. "I will not charge for the lessons. And he can practice here. But he must never play in public without my permission."

Johannes was in bed. His nose twitched. What was that strange smell? Smoke. He ran to the window. A big cloud of black smoke hung over the roofs of the houses in the distance. Then a burst of flames lit up the early morning sky. The Great Fire of Hamburg in 1842 raged for three whole days. Johannes couldn't get to Mr. Cossel's house for his music lessons. No matter which street he tried, the fire blocked his path.

"I haven't tried this way," said Johannes and began walking down a narrow alley. Suddenly he saw a sign. "Baumgarten & Heinz – piano factory." The door was open so he went inside.

"Who have we here?" It was the deep voice of Mr. Baumgarten, the owner of the factory.

Johannes was scared.

"My name is Johannes Brahms, Sir."

"Do you play the piano, Johannes Brahms?" asked Mr. Baumgarten.

"Yes, but we don't have one at home," replied Johannes.

"Let me hear you play," said Mr. Baumgarten. Johannes began to play. All the craftsmen put down their tools and listened. When Johannes finished playing, everyone applauded.

"From now on you can practice here," said Mr. Baumgarten.

At school, Johannes was exhausted. Again last night his father had taken him to play in a noisy bar at the waterfront. His father had begged Mr. Cossel for permission because they really needed the money.

As soon as school was over, Johannes hurried to the factory to practice. Soon he was to play in a competition. The winner would travel to America to give concerts. Johannes was determined to win. Then they would never have to worry about money again.

Mrs. Brahms was worried. Where was Johannes? He should be home by now. She heard a noise in the street below. A large wagon was standing in the middle of the road and a crowd had gathered around it. Mrs. Brahms went down the stairs. There she saw her husband, carrying Johannes in his arms.

For weeks Johannes lay in bed. His legs hurt where the heavy wagon wheels had run over him. But the tears in his eyes were not from the pain. He wasn't strong enough to play the piano. Could he win the competition without practicing?

"Johannes won, Mr. Cossel." Jakob Brahms was so excited. "We're going to America."

"America?" Mr. Cossel was angry. "The boy is not ready. He is only ten years old. My own teacher, Eduard Marxsen, is in town. If he will teach Johannes, will you give up this crazy idea?"

Mr. Cossel hurried to Professor Marxsen's studio and explained about Johannes.

"My only hope is that you will agree to teach him."

"Bring him to me," said Professor Marxsen.

"Such a small boy!" he said when he saw
Johannes. "Can you play this for me?" Eagerly,
Johannes sat down at the piano and began to play.

"First lesson tomorrow at two o'clock!" announced Professor Marxsen without hesitation.

"May I bring you some of my own music?" asked Johannes.

"Of course. Bring it along. I will help you to compose."

Johannes Brahms went to bed early that night. Tomorrow he would show his music to Professor Marxsen. Tomorrow he would start to become a composer.

As an old man, Johannes Brahms burned a lot of his music on a huge bonfire. He wanted to make sure that all the music left behind after he died would be perfect for everyone to hear. Brahms left four symphonies, two piano concertos, a violin concerto, a double concerto for violin and cello, and many beautiful songs.

Brahms loved gypsy music and composed exciting Hungarian Dances.

Today, children still fall asleep to the beautiful sound of the Brahms Lullaby.